REA

# Motorcycle Drag Racing

By Martin Hintz and Kate Hintz

**Reading Consultant:**
Chris Kalifeiz
American Motorcyclist

C A P S T O N E    P R E S S
M A N K A T O ,    M I N N E S O T A

# CAPSTONE PRESS
## 818 North Willow Street • Mankato, MN 56001

Printed in the United States of America.

*Library of Congress Cataloging-in-Publication Data*
Hintz, Martin.
    Motorcycle drag racing/by Martin and Kate Hintz
    p. cm. -- (Drag racing)
    Includes bibliographical references and index.
    Summary: Describes motorcycle dragsters and their sport; includes a history.
    ISBN 1-56065-387-6
    1. Motorcycle racing--Juvenile literature. 2. Drag racing--Juvenile literature [1. Motorcycle racing. 2. Drag racing.] I. Hintz, Kate. II. Title. III. Series: Drag racing (Mankato, Minn.)
GV1060.H56 1996
796.7'5--dc20

                                        96-22338
                                         CIP
                                          AC

Photo credits
John Boykin, 12. FPG/Jeffrey Sylvester, 20.Motorcycle Magazine, 4, 8, 10,14-24, 28, 30, 34-38, 42. Max Scherwin, 6, 26, 33, 41. Victory Associates, cover.

# Table of Contents

Words in **boldface** type in the text are defined
in the Glossary in the back of this book.

# *Chapter 1*

# Motorcycle Drag Racing

In a motorcycle drag race, two motorcycles race at a time. They race down a short, straight, concrete track. They race against the clock. Each rider wants to get the best time.

Drag races are tests of **acceleration**. The motorcycles start from a complete stop. They reach speeds over 200 miles (320 kilometers) per hour in less than 10 seconds.

## Points

Riders receive points for their place in each event. They receive points if they qualify at major races called nationals. Points are given

**In a drag race, two motorcycles race at a time.**

for being the highest qualifier in the world finals.

The rider with the most points at the end of the year is the world champion in his or her **class**. In case of a tie, extra credit is given for winning the most races.

## Favorite Cycles

Riders like to call their motorcycles bikes or cycles. They have favorite cycles. Some think the American-built Harley-Davidson motorcycles are the best. Others like Japanese bikes made by Kawasaki, Honda, Yamaha, or Suzuki.

Drag-racing cycles are very expensive. Almost every part is **custom-made**.

## Nationals

The Rebel Nationals are held each April in Atlanta, Georgia. The Pingel Thunder Nationals are held each June in Indianapolis,

**Some racers think Harley-Davidsons are the best bikes.**

Indiana. There are many other nationals throughout the year.

Since 1964, the Atco Speedway in New Jersey has hosted the Orient Express U.S. Motorcycle Nationals. Manufacturers show off new bikes and engines there.

## Champions

During the 1995 U.S. Motorcycle Nationals, John Myers set a record. He raced down the quarter-mile (400-meter) track in 7.489 seconds. He lost in a second event.

Myers did not give up. He set another record at the World Finals in Gainesville, Florida. He made it down the track in 7.439 seconds. He won the world championship.

Riders might win one race and lose the next one. It happens all the time in the fast world of drag racing. Part of the thrill is seeing who will be the champion at the end of the year.

**Fans never know who will be the winner in a drag race.**

# *Chapter 2*

# **History**

Drag racing started in the 1930s. Drivers in Southern California raced hot rods. A hot rod is a car that has been **souped up**.

Races went from stoplight to stoplight. Whoever made it to the end of the block first was the winner. These early drag races were not very safe. There were many accidents.

There is a big difference between driving on the street and driving on a racetrack. A street often has potholes and other hazards. An approved track is clear of oil, grease, and **debris**.

**Unlike city streets, racetracks are clear of debris.**

## Safe Tracks

Drag racers looked for safer places. They raced in the desert and at old airfields. A quarter mile (400 meters) was found to be the best distance for a race. A car could go all out in that distance without damaging its engine.

In 1951, the National Hot Rod Association (NHRA) was organized. The NHRA set safety standards for racing. It established events around the country.

## Motorcycle Drags

Many people in the 1930s rode motorcycles, too. They were less expensive than the hot rods.

Early cyclists liked to race as much as the hot rodders. They souped up their motorcycles. They also had trouble finding safe places to race.

The NHRA included motorcycles in the 1960s. The association helped find tracks for

The NHRA sanctions drag racing events across the country.

motorcycle drag racing. Rules were established.

## Motorcycle Associations

Today, the American Motorcyclists Association (AMA) **sanctions** races for Kawasaki, Yamaha, Suzuki, and Honda motorcycles. The AMA has only a few classes for Harley-Davidson cycles.

Harleys are made in Milwaukee, Wisconsin. The American Motorcycle Racing Association (AMRA) was formed just for Harley racers.

The International Drag Bike Association (IDBA) holds events for every type of bike. Riders know that events sanctioned by any of these organizations will be safe and well run.

**Officials from the sanctioning associations inspect the motorcycles before they are allowed to race.**

# *Chapter 3*

# **The Drag Race**

B oth motorcycle and automobile drag races have similar tracks and rules. The drag strip is always a straight stretch of concrete. A line painted down the middle of the track divides it into two lanes.

Cycles race two at a time. The winner advances to the next round. Rounds continue until only one cycle remains. The winning rider is called the top eliminator.

## Two Types of Racing

There are two types of motorcycle drag racing. One is called heads-up racing. In this

**In heads-up racing, the first driver to reach the finish line wins.**

type, the first racer to reach the finish line wins.

The other type of racing is called bracket racing. In this type of racing, racers receive an average time in **preliminary trials**. They try to match that time in the actual races.

In bracket races, racers try to be consistent. They want to get the same time in each race. If they go faster or slower than their average time, they might lose.

## The Burnout Box and Timing Tower

Amateur and professional riders race the same way. They start in the burnout box. This is where they burn oil and other debris off the rear tire to get better traction. The rider revs the engine, spinning the back tire until it is clean.

In the early days of drag racing, bleach was poured under the back tires before the riders burned them off. But bleach often overheated

**In the burnout box, riders spin their back tire to clear it of debris.**

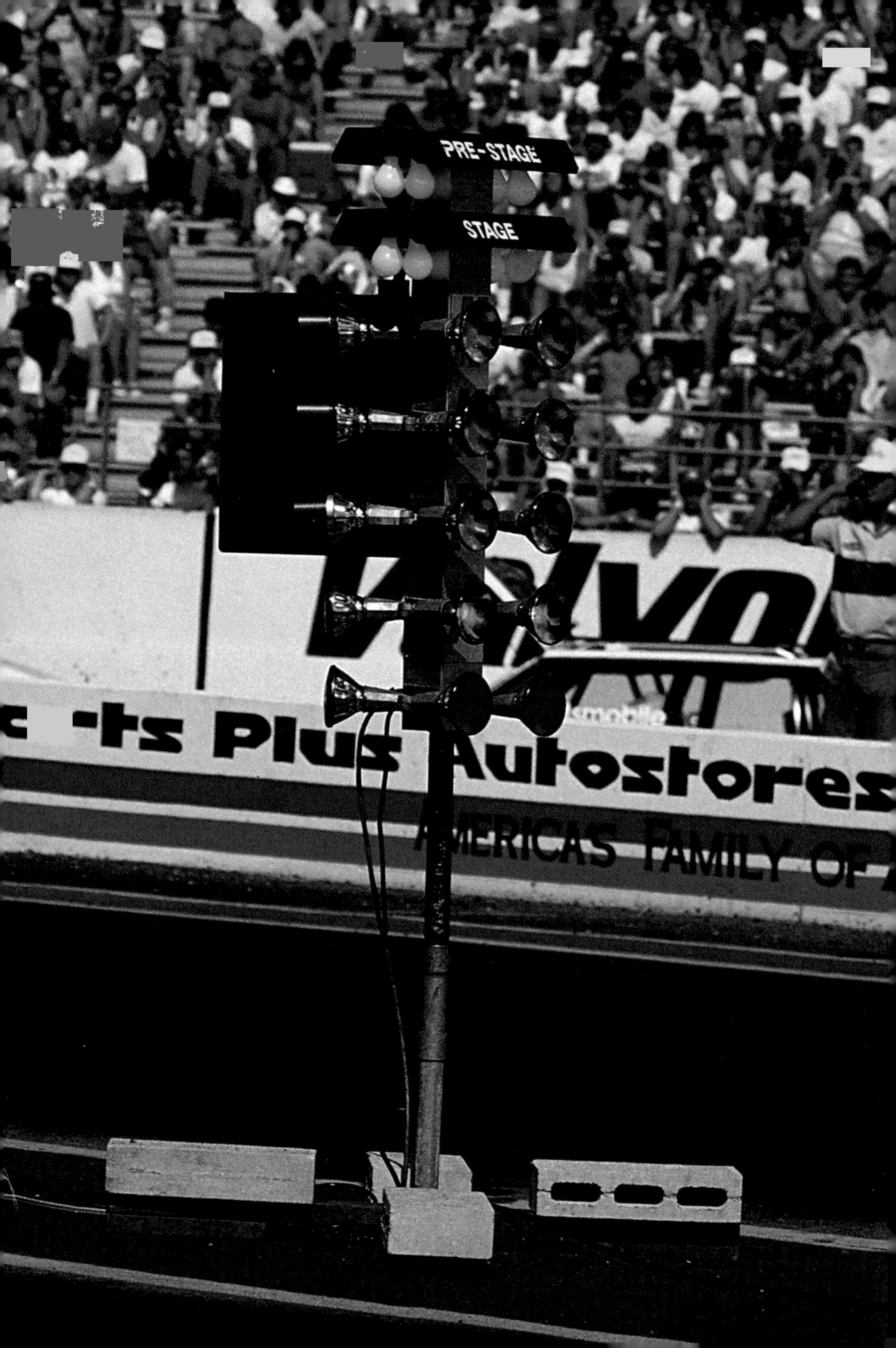
PRE-STAGE
STAGE
-ts Plus Autostores
AMERICAS FAMILY OF

and caused fires. Today, a mixture of water and chemicals is used instead of bleach.

Timers and race officials watch the race from the timing tower. This is a tall building between the race lanes. The computers that record the times are in the tower.

## The Christmas Tree

A pole called the Christmas tree sits between the two racing lanes. It is 20 feet (six meters) ahead of the starting line. There are two rows of red, yellow, and green lights on the tree. There is a row for each cycle.

The top yellow light tells the racers to go to the starting line. The second yellow light goes on when the motorcycles are in position and ready to start the race.

Next are three more sets of yellow lights. These tell racers to get ready. Next is a green light. When it signals, the riders start the race. If the red light goes on, it means one rider started too soon. That rider is **disqualified**.

**A pole between the racing lanes called a Christmas tree tells the racers when to get ready and when to go.**

**After each race, mechanics fine-tune the engine for the next race.**

The motorcycles are timed with electric beams. These are located at the starting and finish lines. The time it takes a bike to cross both beams is called the elapsed time or e.t.

## Professional Timing

In professional races, timing is measured at three points. The first time is taken 60 feet from the starting line. The next time is taken halfway down the track. The third time is taken at the finish line.

These times are studied after a race. Racers compare them to times from earlier races. They can see where they need to improve.

## After the Race

A safety crew waits at the end of the track. If there is a crash, a cycle's fuel tank could explode and cause a fire. The safety crew has equipment to put out fires.

The rider's crew brings the cycle back to the **pit** area. There, mechanics fine-tune or rebuild the engine.

Racers keep records on each race. After the racing season, the records show how well the cycle performed.

# Chapter 4
# Kinds of Racing

All racing is broken into classes. Each class is for a different style of motorcycle. This makes the competition fair.

The highest professional class is called top fuel. These are the fastest cycles in the world. They produce massive **horsepower**.

Top fuelers burn a fuel called nitromethane. Other cycles use ordinary gasoline. Chemicals are sometimes added to the gasoline. They make the cycles go faster. The chemicals are called exciters.

**Top fuelers are the fastest motorcycles in the world.**

**Drivers keep records on each race.**

### Pro Modified and Pro Stock

Another professional class is called pro modified. In the pro modified class, no cycle is the same. They are all **customized**. Sometimes only one piece of original equipment remains on a cycle.

Another professional class is called pro stock. In the pro stock class, the cycles look like they were bought at a dealer. But the engine is much more powerful than dealer bikes.

The top fuel, pro modified, and pro stock classes are run only at national events.

## E.T. Racing

Another class is called e.t. racing or **handicap** racing. There are both professional and amateur e.t. races.

In an e.t. race, slower cycles have a chance to beat faster ones. The slower cycle gets a head start. How much of a head start is determined during practice **heats**.

After several practice heats, racers arrive at an average speed. The head start is the difference between the slower rider's average speed and the faster rider's average speed.

## Dial-In Times

A racer's average speed from the practice heats is called a dial-in time. Say one racer's dial-in time is 10.00 seconds. Say the other racer has a dial-in time of 9.50 seconds. This means that the first racer will get the green light .50 seconds before the other racer.

**Sponsors put their logos all over the motorcycles.**

If both motorcycles ran their dial-in times, they would arrive at the finish line at the same time. This does not happen very often, though. One cycle usually gets to the finish first. But using dial-in times makes the races fair.

Thousands of riders compete at tracks across the United States and Canada. There are even drag strips on the Caribbean islands. Only a few racers become top professionals, though. Most racers are amateurs.

## Sponsors

Racing is expensive. Racing teams have to pay for travel, food, lodging, and equipment. Sometimes they need new engines. If there is a crash, they might need a whole new bike.

Sponsors contribute money to racing teams to help pay for expenses. Sponsors are oil companies, motorcycle equipment manufacturers, or other businesses. They put their logos on the cycles. Often, a racer's uniform is covered with sponsor logos.

Supporting a winning racer is good advertising for a business. Sponsors want to be thought of as the choice of the champions. Then they can sell more of their products to both racers and racing fans.

# Chapter 5

# Safe Racing

Safety is important in drag racing. Every racer wears a helmet. The helmets have visors to protect the eyes. Helmets and clothing must meet standards set by the racing organizations.

Racers wear leather jackets, leather gloves, and leather boots that go above the ankle. Leather protects riders if there is an accident. Tennis shoes are not worn. They would be torn to shreds if they scraped the track.

Tires wear out quickly. They are changed often. Some riders put on new tires for each race. They do not want a worn tire to blow out.

**Racers wear leather jackets, leather gloves, and helmets.**

## Kill Switch

All racing cycles have a kill switch. It cuts off the engine if the driver tumbles or loses control.

The kill switch is a **lanyard**. It is made of rawhide or wire. One end is attached to the cycle's ignition. The other end is attached to the rider's wrist. The engine shuts off when the lanyard is pulled.

These safety features work. From 1967 to 1995, only four deaths occurred in motorcycle drag racing at sanctioned events. In case of emergencies, though, there is a medical team at every track.

## Inspections

Motorcycles must meet certain standards. Regulations spell out how thick the metal frames must be and how each frame has to be welded. They regulate how much space there must be between the frame and the ground.

Before a race, safety officials check the frame, tires, and engine. They check each racer's safety gear.

**Drag-racing tires wear out quickly. They must be changed often.**

If a safety officer finds a problem with a cycle, the team mechanics must fix it or change it. If they do not, they are not allowed to race. Every rider is treated the same.

## Other Safety Features

A neutral gear is what allows street bikes to idle in place when the **clutch** is not disengaged. Riders of racing motorcycles must always be seated on them when the engine is running.

Wheelie bars are mounted on the most powerful cycles. They stop a cycle's front wheel from rising too high. If the wheel rises too high, the cycle can flip over and land on a rider.

## Aim Straight

Racers must aim their bikes straight ahead at the starting line. A cycle that is not aimed properly can drift to one side and crash.

If a cycle starts to drift, skilled racers gun the throttle to bring their bikes back under control. Hitting the brakes would make the bikes swerve more.

**Wheelie bars stop the most powerful cycles' front wheels from rising too high.**

**Christmas Tree**

**Wheelie Bars**

**Racing Lane**

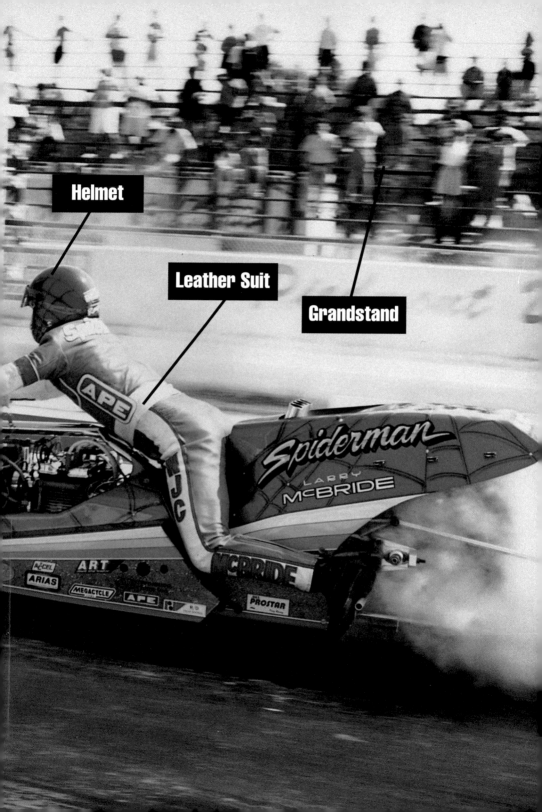

**Helmet**

**Leather Suit**

**Grandstand**

# Chapter 6

# Track Speedsters

Elmer Trett has competed in more than 1,000 races. He reached 234 miles (374 kilometers) per hour on his cycle in 1994. His nitromethane-burning engine produced 1,000 horsepower. He ran the quarter mile (400 meters) in 6.2 seconds.

Trett also designs drag-racing motorcycles. He looks for ways to increase performance. Trett moved his **headers** to a new position near the front wheel. Moving the headers gave Trett more traction and better control.

**Elmer Trett is one of motorcycle drag racing's popular champions.**

**Good riders learn as much as they can. They know that knowledge and experience will help them win.**

racing cycle. She enjoyed it so much, she went on to earn her license in professional motorcycle drag racing. She was the first woman to do so.

Marianne Mylan is another drag racer. She is an executive at the Jamaica Hospital Medical Center in Queens, New York.

The hospital has a special unit that treats traumatic brain injuries. It helps many patients injured in motorcycle accidents. The hospital sponsors Mylan's bike in racing events. She shows her bike at schools and malls and talks about safety.

## Reggie Showers

When Reggie Showers was 10, his dad gave him a Honda dirt bike. When he was 14, Showers was severly shocked by electricity. He lost both of his feet.

Showers still wanted to ride motorcycles. He never gave up his dream. Today, Showers is one of the top motorcycle drag racers.

Showers won the 1989 drag bike world championship. He was only 25 years old. In 1995, Showers was hired to race full time for Harry Lartigue, owner of a pro-stock Suzuki. Showers has set many records. In his spare time, he flies airplanes.

Showers and other good riders know that it is important to understand the mechanics of racing. They learn as much as they can by getting their hands dirty working on equipment. That knowledge helps them win.

# Glossary

**acceleration**—the rate at which something changes speeds

**class**—separate category for different styles of motorcycles

**clutch**—a part that transfers power from the engine to the wheels

**custom-made**—made to fit a single special order

**customized**—change a vehicle to fit one's own tastes or needs

**debris**—bits and pieces of litter

**disqualify**—kick out of a race

**handicap**—when a disadvantage is put on a racer to make the race more competitive

**header**—a single pipe that brings two or more pipes together to carry exhaust from the engine

**heat**— preliminary rounds of a race

**horsepower**—a unit used to measure the power of engines and motors

**lanyard**—a cord or rope used for fastening

**pit**—area away from the racetrack where mechanics work on motorcycles
**preliminary trials**—another name for heats
**sanction**—officially approve
**soup up**—to increase an engine's power

# To Learn More

**Connolly, Maureen.** *Dragsters*. Mankato, Minn.: Capstone Press, 1992.

**Nentl, Jerolyn Ann.** *Drag Racing*. Mankato, Minn.: Crestwood House, 1979.

**Puleo, Nicole.** *Drag Racing*. Minneapolis: Lerner, 1973.

**Smith, Jay.** *Drag Racing*. Minneapolis: Capstone Press, 1995.

You can read more about drag racing in *Junior Drag Racer* magazine.

# Useful Addresses

**American Motorcyclists Association**
33 Collegeview Road
Westerville, OH 43081-1484

**Canadian Motorcycle Association**
500 James Street North #201
Hamilton, ON L8L 8C4
Canada

**National Hod Rod Association Motorcycle Division**
P.O. Box 555
Glendora, CA 91740-0950

**Prostar Drag Racing**
P.O. Box 18039
Huntsville, AL 35804

# Internet Sites

**Cycle News**
http://www.cyclenews.com/

**Drag Racing & Hi Performance Illustrated**
http://www.dragracer.com/

**Motorcycle Racing InfoCentre**
http://gil.ipswichcity.qld.gov.au/~wildlife/

**NHRA Online**
http://www.goracing.com/nhra/

# Index